TRAVELING LIGHT

Traveling Light

poems

NORMA ALMQUIST

FITHIAN PRESS
SANTA BARBARA, 1997

Some of these poems originally appeared in
Yes, Focus, Crosscurrents, Epos,
Morning in Her Shoes, New Orleans Review,
and *Traveling Without a Camera*

Published by Fithian Press
A division of Daniel and Daniel, Publishers, Inc.
Post Office Box 1525
Santa Barbara, CA 93102

Design by Eric Larson

LIBRARY OF CONGRESS CATALOGING-IN-PUBLICATION DATA
Almquist, Norma.
    Traveling light : poems / by Norma Almquist
        p.   cm.
    ISBN 1-56474-192-3 (alk. paper)
    I. Title
PS3551.L56T73   1997
811'.54—dc20   96-20476
                                                  CIP

*To my family
and to Jeanne Nichols, who went there, too*

Contents

TRAVELING LIGHT

Last Chance?

One of my brains requires travel,
another one huddles at home.
One of them starts to unravel
when it loses its contact with loam.

So travel, homemaking, and gardening
are the trio that governs my life.
For a person whose innards are hardening,
this makes for considerable strife.

On which shall I spend my last vigor?
On the world, on the house, on the dirt?
If I compound them all with fierce rigor,
I could grow camel food near my yurt.

Vacation

Each day opens like a peach
full of sun and the sweetness
of silence and space
and the freedom just to be
awesome gifts
that everyone deserves

Going Overland

We headed toward something
at a modest pace
hoping to be found

All around us
was home
for somebody

We looked into
one another's eyes
where language hides

How far,
we would have said,
at the stone-sided well
sunk in the savannah
In the red-dusty tea stall
that smelled of camel
By the twig fire
under the pygmy moon
How far?

Here, said the bread,
baking on the stone
Here, said the child,
holding up the sun
Here, the wheels whispered
Here   Here

Selifke

In a tent, by a boatless harbor,
we looked out at the castle, floating
on a clear jade sea
facing Rhodes.

Sultans and crusaders
whispered in the air around us,
"We were lovers too. Remember.
Rage and boast

and cold abstractions
stole the scent of plums and warm skin,
fouled our feelings and transformed us,
young, to ghosts."

From our tent we watched the castle,
a golden toy for princes, both
a target and a weapon. We held
each other close.

"I Could Have Seen This on TV"

Another place he didn't like at all
was Nepal.
All those hills
made him feel quite ill.
"Travel is a pain,"
he said, "one damn plane
after another.
Why bother?
I like to be
where people know me."

Istanbul

When you first see the Hagia Sophia
you just can't believe there could be a
building so plump and so gorgeous.
We stand with our guide, eager for lore. Just
inside the door our shoes wait for us.
They look familiar and strange.
God seems to be everywhere.

Central African Republic

His young black skin was shining and wet
from the pool where I saw him
the green leaves bent toward him
red blossoms behind them

His curved jet back bent gracefully down
toward the foot he was washing
the dark water touched him
warm air slid around him

The rough red track led past him so quickly
so quickly he vanished
his present our past
the garden soon lost

Airline Food

Maybe fasting is the thing
to do.
Forget that gray lump
called chicken and the glue
that hides it. That's gravy?
Forget the limp lettuce,
the stone roll, the whole mess.

After all,
not even a bird will eat
at 30,000 feet.

Teotihuacan

Think of falling off the pyramid!
The very thought'll
wipe every bit of Nahuatl
out of your mind.
So much for night school.
Best to travel
where your learning won't unravel.

Benares

Think of a place
that is always quiet,
where stillness is the breath
of the city,
the stillness of minds meditating,
the stillness of the dead,
wrapped tight and carried
on bony shoulders
down to the river.
Even the screech
of traffic in the jammed streets,
of monkeys in the temple trees
falls soft against such stillness
and partakes.
Nothing, it seems to say,
is solely itself.

Be Careful

The thing about the Sahara
is that you have to care a
lot about camels.
Camels are mean.
If they don't sit on you,
they spit on you.
Take plenty of water.

The Journey

I'm seeking what I used to know,
behind the temple, in a dream,
sing me, sing me, song, rejoice me,

Going where I used to go,
through the forest, to the rim,
send me, send me, path, extend me,

Through the labyrinth, to the cave,
to the waters under mountains,

Where the knower and the known
merge into that single one
spirit, mind, or essence clear,
and everything is everywhere.

Stick to a Light Diet

The rice cakes are plumper
in Kuala Lumpur.
When you're there, it's nice
to eat nothing but rice.
If you don't the fish you had
will make you wish you had.

"But I Like It"

A man from L.A. took the red-eye
and landed in London for the first time.
The grass was more green
than he'd ever seen.
The Brits were so charming
he found them alarming.

Things were so strange.
He found a whole range
of oddities:
sausage rolls, beans on toast,
misty days, pebbly coasts,
roundabouts, snooker halls,
bitter pints. Where are the malls?

The words that came to him to say
on postcards he mailed to friends each day?
"This is absolutely, definitely not L.A."

A Wonder of the World

What if when you saw the Taj Mahal
you didn't like it at all.
What if you thought it was too round
and cold and white
and didn't like the idea of such a great tomb
swelling up like that at night.
Wouldn't people think you were vulgar,
insensitive—a boor?
Let's not talk about it anymore.

Near Bangui—Central African Republic

A woman pounds millet
lifts the long pole high
above her shoulders
plunges it into the mortar
again   again   again

In her thin useful body
hair bound in bright cotton
she pounds through the fresh morning hours
work that comes back each dawn
labelled Woman

Early Morning—Bali

rib-thumping roosters
crack the dawn
with echoing cries

chicks of all colors
scuttle and tumble
near jittery hens

flat-footed ducks
troop after a man
with a flag on a pole

jut-ribbed dogs
lick rice from offerings
laid on the ground

villagers carry
gifts for the gods
—like flowers walking

Traveling Light

On the Chattahoochee River
near the Apalachicola
is where alligators flick
their fiendish tails

On the beach at Pondicherry
not too far from Cuddalore
there's a man who sleeps upon
a bed of nails

O the world is round and full and packed
with wonders to behold
and I want to see all I can see
before I get too old

When you're close to Um da Fogg
and your camel's getting tired
you and he can rest beneath
the baobab

In the jungle on the way to
Bosobolo muddy hippos
lie along the banks of rivers
catching cod

On the way to Karakorum
you will pass through Srinagar
where they all keep charcoal fires
beneath their skirts

In the far Mongolian desert
people riding tiny ponies
will serve you buttered tea
inside their yurts

O the world is round and full and packed
with wonders to behold
and I want to see all I can see
before I get too old

Through a canyon past a mountain
you will come to Wadi Rumm
where children dance their goats
across the sand

On a small Pacific island
Pingelap or Satawal
you can watch a tattooed sailor
lead a band

If your elephant leaves you stranded
on the Hoogly River shore
ride a tiger to the Little
Rann of Kutch

If when you get to Nan Madol
the stones fly through the sky
you can be a little scared
but not too much

O the world is round and full and packed
with wonders to behold
and I want to see all I can see
before I get too old

I have heard that birds fly backwards
at the bottom of the world
that the dogs in Patagonia
are flat

that a man in Ouagadougou
has a snake that sings offkey
and a woman in Bihar lives
in her hat

O the world is round and full and packed
with wonders to behold
and I want to see all I can see
before I get too old too old
before I get too old

Wind Song

Sometimes I dream of
the Chinook, Sirocco, Mistral, and the Föhn,
winds that blow wild in the world,
winds that no knowledge or technique can tame.
(They're probably girls.)

They drive people mad if they linger too long.
Their hot breath heats blood and stirs wrath.
If you think you can handle them, careful—you're wrong.
Stay out of their path.

We have one at home that is gaining in fame,
a world-class, roaring wild thing.
The desert her father, Santa Ana her name,
she's out for a fling.

So I browse through the atlas and dream of away,
of forces beyond what I know.
But home has its weathers that power each day.
I guess I won't go.

Sleeping in the Station:
Jhansi, Uttar Pradesh

She sleeps with her back to me,
an old thin woman in a green sari.
A few inches of cement floor
separate the islands our mats make.

Rain rattles the roof,
roils up scents that are, in memory, proof
of home—urine, dung, cow...
a farm in Iowa warms my mind.

But a little boy, here and now,
pees in the corner. A sacred cow,
blonde and self-absorbed, nudges
the door, munches someone's chapatti.

We rustle in our clothes and sigh
when the harsh lights go out. Babies cry
softly; children murmur. A father
tiptoes in, finds somehow the island

his family makes on the floor,
squats down, whispers, then slips out the door.
Even the little mouse
nosing at my feet
is tired. We all sleep.

Thinking of Africa

Thinking of Africa
has brought us here
into this plummy light at dawn
the flat map transformed
by will and desire
into this moment in Sudan

All around us is happening
thorn trees   a robed woman
riding sideways on a donkey
a clay waterjar in her arms
four camels plodding loose-kneed
across the red earth
a baobab
large as a mad dream village
wearing birds   a dark man
carrying a spear and riding
a brown cow
all at home in themselves

we brush past one another
like corpuscles in the vast
body of God

we make our small fires
brew tea and watch
the mother of us all
come back from the dark

this could be home

Economy Flight—L.A./London

Okay. I'll take the middle.
After a couple thousand miles it'll
seem normal to hunch here and stare
at the gritty thatch of hair
rising out of the seat before me.
Who needs to see
Greenland. Icebergs. The Irish coast.
I'll just hunker down and make the most
of where I am.
Let's face it. The most is damn
little.
I hate the middle.

Don't Miss It

I went to Turkey
ignorant as a stone.
Carpets and harems
were all I'd ever known.

"Troy is here? That big wooden horse
isn't Greek? Okay, Greek, but stranded
so far from home?"

And remember the Ephesians?
Ephesus is right there,
cobbled streets, temples,
library and all....
You can almost hear Saint Paul.

There, too,
tucked under a great tree,
is the small house
where the Virgin Mary
may have lived her last days.

Not to mention the Blue Mosque,
the Hagia Sophia and the Bosphorus,
apple orchards fragrant
under the bluest sky,
and country cafes
made of one rickety table,
two chairs, a shade tree,
and a pot of chai.

Yes, Turkey
is something to see.

Geography 101 or Whatever Happened to the Tributaries of the Nile

Soil is creeping down the hill
In a regolithian spill
There are horsts and grabens
standing side by side.

Though moraines invade the talus
Scarps and screes will never quail us
Long as there's a karst around
In which to hide.

Oh, the aa it is growing
And the facts are clearly showing
That pahoehoe is increasing
Ever more.

The diastrophic spasms
Bring on fissures, faults, and chasms
And felsenmeer lies scattered
Near the tor.

Oh, the anticlines are rising
And it's not at all surprising
That monadnocks shyly masquerade
as hills.

When the magma starts extruding
It's no time to be intruding
On a landscape that is
Obviously ill.

How the world has changed for me
since I take Geography
I can't recognize a
Once familiar view.

These odd facts are worth ingestion
But I do have one small question
Won't I ever learn
The products of Peru?

World

World, that snug egg,
sky-capped
chocked with gems,
juices, jingling
as it spins, birds
falling out of trees,
flashing red, green, gold;
flowers flying, flinging
scents of spring, of sun,
of singing
here and there and
careless splendor
everywhere something
dances, glints, soars
endless seeming the
roaring richness,
it rolls, snug egg,
nestled in its galaxy

Don't break.

What Next?

I have a friend who goes traveling
in regions most travelers would dread.
Is she seeking out knowledge or wisdom?
No, she's looking for new kinds of bread.

Chapattis, tortillas, and pitas
make the hardships of travel a lark.
The flat loaves that Bedouins blacken
in fires make the desert a park.

Puris light up a Kashmiri morning,
in Caracas arepas taste right,
and bannocks are perfect to munch on
with her tea through the long Arctic night.

The kisra in Fez scents the Casbah
as Johnny Bakes scent Trinidad,
while the Tuareg in the Sahara
serve tagella that make her heart glad.

So my friend roams the world, always happy,
pursuing her passion with zest,
for she knows, in the most remote corner,
she'll add a new bread to her list.

Wadi Rumm/Jordan

moonlight on Wadi Rumm
lights up the silver fort
lights the black tents
where the Bedouin sleep

soft clang of camel bells
marks where the camels stir
shuffle and sigh
as they sleepily feed

now the last fire is out
only the moon and stars
burn in their dance
we turn in for the night

sunk in our sleeping bags
spread on the desert we
dream ancient dreams
as we spin toward the light

Puzzle

Looking at things...
Joy rising...
sheen of seed
jut of buttock
curve of cheek   thigh   tawny hill
space spilling past time

Why what is not me or mine
exalts me
is a human secret.
No iris ever found me beautiful.

Transatlantic Flight

Greenland dreams below, all silent.
Round eyes, brown in the bushes,
brood above a leaf.

Icebergs, in stately dance, take
centuries to unform.

We nest in our sealed pod,
scuffing among papers,
sucking on private sounds,
drowsing along the curve of the earth…

The pod drifts to land, cracks;
we scatter,
riding our secret winds.

Maybe Later

To travel, they say, is so charming,
so with it, so cool, and so chic.
If you're someone who finds it alarming,
keep quiet. Deny that you're meek,

that strange places, strange food and behavior
make you want to crawl under the bed,
that travel cannot be your saviour,
if you're sure you'd be better off dead.

When vacation time comes and you're queried
by friends and relations, "Where to?"
In a voice that is blasé and wearied,
say, "I've seen it all, haven't you?"

The Atoll

The atoll, a drifting star
in a universe of blues,
nestled in the language
of a few hundred people
who had named it into being.

One of them knelt by the firepit,
her brown breasts pointing toward
the buried coals.
We wove palm fronds
into plates and lined them
with leaves,
ready for the baked taro.

Vowels and soft consonants
melded in the air around us
like the brush of birds' wings
and the lapping reef.

A girl straddled
the grating stool, rubbed
split coconuts over
its serrated neck and sang.
Small fish browned
on the open fire.

Home was here, and music.
Dancers and stars moved
across the night as always.

The young man walked to
the canoe house,
stroked the prow of the outrigger,
stared out past the reef.
"Other," he said, in the new
language he had heard.
"Other."

Sphinx with Pyramids

The tour buses line the road above.
Tourists spill out and flow down
toward the Sphinx and restaurant,
eddying here and there around
clumps of souvenir merchants
and renters of camels.
Just before sunset
camels with tourists
and tourists without camels
plod toward the pyramids.
All those big feet
in the bony sand.

River Journey

Some people purr up the Nile,
cold drinks and video camera steady,
their Love Boat captain and Visa card ready
to lead them to an experience
worth photographing.

We drifted up, or scuttled, as the wind chose.
Our fellucca breathed and shifted on the water. We
lay on our stomachs on the hot wood. Freed
from the dam, the tamed clear water brushed
our fingers. Even so, we felt history.

Bedouin Camp—Jordan

Sticks hold the scrap of wool
the child has made into a tent,
a six-inch echo of her family's tent
that stretches behind her like a
great black wing.

Soft Arabic sounds she makes
corral the tiny goats,
fashioned from twigs and wool balls.
Her father rides past, a young camel
lashed down in the bed
of his Toyota pickup.

Simple Declarative

The earth breathes beneath the pavement.
I hear it.

Mountains wait for me.
Grass is getting impatient.
Some flowers have already left.

A bird is sitting in my head,
but he is not singing.

Something is waiting.
I'd better go.

Classification at Evening

A swirl of birds
has swept across
the sky.

A yawp of puppies
nags me
with its cry.

A swank of penguins
just went sauntering
by.   (I swear.)
A rout of flies
is causing me
to lie

inside the screened-in porch
a crunch of carpenters
put up the other day.

A rube of farmhands
standing tensely
by

a swoon of virgins
(who are set
to cry

out "yes" and "no"
at once) just then
descries

me lurking in
the darkened porch
and tries

to look as cool
as any
sneak of spies.

I wipe away
my look of mild surmise;

a croon of nightingales
sings
lullabies.

I close my eyes.

Lesson

The mountains declare
that space once filled
is rarely stable.

Birds remind us
that space is movement,
movement, time.

Here and now
is both redundant
and profound,
beyond us earthbound,
haunted, Eden-seekers.

Thus we plow our way,
following what's behind,
leaning on air.

How Far

Yes, I've been to Bora Bora.
Even now, it seems more a
dream than a real place.

Colors saturate the senses.
Turquoise, royal blue, jade flood the fences
dim habits have built.

Jagged fairy-tale peaks, furred green, rise
narrow and pointed as a magician's cap. Skies
helplessly blue hold perfect clouds.

Tourists on the beach read books,
their gaze inward, their scant look
around lamed by fiction.

The sacred world shimmers around us,
each object perfect in itself, loose
and knowing, how to be

not a question. How far do we have to go
to learn what a stone knows,
what water tells.

Knowledge

"I take these stones to be
petrified sheep," said the old man
in the vicinity of Marathon.

"I take these stones to be
proof of love and fidelity," I said
in the vicinity of marriage.

Archaeologists and anthropologists
smiled.

My Old Woman

I'm shaping my old woman, I would say,
starting for a solitary walk.
I carry her inside, a print, a clock,
an image to be carved out of the clay

that I am wearing. So I start to pare
away the fat, the flab that blurs the line,
and solitude is just the place to hone
the leading edge that juts out to the stare

of space, of age, of what else I don't know.
I'll walk until I pass beyond the need
for softness, the touch beneath what's said;
I'll try to follow where I need to go.

My old woman stirs inside my skin,
tough, lucid, edgy, revelling in what's here.
Her eyes look out through mine, confront the stare;
we start to walk out past where we have been.

At the Beach on Sunday

Naked in our flawed flesh
we wear our failures of will and taste
        and dream of Eden

Fallen under the eyes of gods
we lie against the skin of earth
        and dream of Eden

        (if i'm sexy   if i travel   if i learn a lot)

Images of perfection
wheel like shooting gallery ducks
behind our eyes

The sun blunts its rays against our guarded skin
the wine-dark sea is a toy for the kids

Micronesia I

The thing about Micronesia
is that if you sneeze you
miss an island or two.
If you go at all,
think small.

Micronesia II

Imagine a country where the money
is bigger than the people,
not philosophically or politically
(like here)
but physically, weightily, more dear.
Try holding a hundred dollars in your lap
on Yap.

Micronesia III

Guam is a place
you could take your mom,
especially if she's Japanese.
The water along the beach
is jade and shallow.
Honeymooners from Tokyo reach
for another squirt of suntan lotion
which they stroke onto each other
with tentative, exploratory motion,
their faces calm.
I would guess that
lots of Japanese are made in Guam.

Trail Song

the sea is a cup
the birds drink from
the moon aims her light
at the ridge
the stars form a map
that will lead me home
the wind hangs his breath
from the ledge

my feet on the path
stroke the skin
of the earth
my eyes make her beauty known
the Mother and I
dance our way through the night
happy to be not alone   alone
happy to be not alone

View from Space

See how the Mother sleeps
with the continents in her arms,
her blue robe loosened.

The Father's mind, subtle and secret,
stirs the galaxies,
testing   testing

The children fret and dream,
bide in their bony caves,
reach out through their five doors—
            disappear

Songs are left
colors spread by hands
small lucid vessels

Reply from Algiers

<pre>
yes   the air is new
yes   the Casbah mazes
yes   the women slip along
       in their white cocoons
       who they are
       hidden
       even from themselves
yes   the Sahara waits
       I believe there's an oasis
       in the south
       where butterflies burst out
       from the pregnant light

no   it's not me
       who will come home
</pre>